MARTY CAMDEN

WOODWORKING

The Ultimate Beginner's Guide to Woodworking, Learn About the Basics and The Essential Woodworking Techniques and Skills to Start Your Own Wood Projects

Descrierea CIP a Bibliotecii Naţionale a României
MARTY CAMDEN
    WOODWORKING. The Ultimate Beginner's Guide to Woodworking, Learn About the Basics and The Essential Woodworking Techniques and Skills to Start Your Own Wood Projects / Marty Camden – Bucharest: Editura My Ebook, 2021
    ISBN

MARTY CAMDEN

WOODWORKING

The Ultimate Beginner's Guide to Woodworking, Learn About the Basics and The Essential Woodworking Techniques and Skills to Start Your Own Wood Projects

My Ebook Publishing House
Bucharest, 2021

TABLE OF CONTENTS

INTRODUCTION

So you're thinking you want to learn woodworking?

Woodworking can be a fun and satisfying hobby, but it can also be quite frustrating. In a world filled with mass- produced, poorly crafted pieces of furniture, it can be a thrill to produce a piece made with your own two hands.

Take a few pieces of wood, some tools, and your imagination, and you can make beautiful pieces of furniture. The possibilities with carpentry are endless. Even the most inexperienced person can learn woodworking and turn out gorgeous pieces that can become heirlooms.

Woodworking as a hobby is growing in popularity – especially among the female population. More and more women are taking a new interest in jig saws and power drills as they turn out accessories and furniture for their homes.

The term "woodworking" literally refers to the process of building, making or carving something using wood. Kind of obvious, isn't it? But there are all types of pieces that can be made using wood – not just furniture! You can make toys, toy boxes, or carved figurines.

It can truly become an art form.

So where and how does an aspiring woodworker begin?

Many people benefit greatly from taking a class at the local college or community center. Others prefer to read a book or magazine. Still others prefer to just jump right in.

There's no one right way to start. It depends on how much experience you have with using the tools essential to woodworking.

Woodworking is not nearly as daunting as it may seem. It is not necessary to spend a fortune on tools and supplies. Many projects can be done with a minimum investment and your imagination!

Woodworking is a huge hobby, with the number of active participants estimated by some within the industry at between seven and eleven million strong. Each brings their own set of capabilities and interests that often make specific techniques more applicable in their situation. As long as the techniques chosen are safe, and produce the desired results, they are right for them.

This book is intended to introduce you to basic woodworking terms, getting started with a stocked shop, carving out your workspace, and introducing you to some basic woodworking projects. We will concentrate mainly in here on building pieces of furniture. Once you get the hang of this, you can get more in-depth with carving, etc. as you learn to better use your tools.

This is not a comprehensive, definitive guide, but a good way to get started crafting your own projects and learning the satisfaction of making your own furniture, toys, and much more!

We've included a section on shop safety, and some easy projects we found to get you started!

So let's start with the newbie's guide to woodworking!

YOUR SPACE

The first thing you need to consider is where you'll be crafting your projects. Most people take up woodworking in their garage or basement. This is fine; just remember that you'll need some space to store materials and the finished product. You'll want a space that is easy to move around in and that you can keep organized.

If you're using power tools, you'll need easily accessible power outlets. Remember that power tools can be quite noisy, so take into consideration the comfort of your family and your neighbors.

You'll need a workbench which doesn't necessarily have to be elaborate. It's a space for you to work on and keep your plans out in the open.

You can buy commercially made workbenches at most home supply stores. When choosing a workbench, look for one with a wood top, or another smooth, non-marking top, so that the surface doesn't scuff the wood you use for your projects. Storage underneath the bench is nice if your budget allows a model with built-in drawers and cabinets.

Choose a workbench that fits comfortably in your shop space and that matches the types of projects you think you'll be working on. A small workbench will do for crafting toys, but you'll need a larger space if you're making armoires.

But you're getting started with woodworking as a hobby. Why not make your own workbench? This will give you valuable experience and will become one of the most useful items in your shop! We've included a simple workbench plan in this book. Try diving right in with and start your workshop out with a piece you made yourself!

It's a good idea to have a bin where you can place operating manuals from your tools. This way, you won't lose them and they'll be easily accessible.

We also recommend a good tool box to store your tools and a box such as a tackle box to sore nails, screws, etc. in.

As with most any projects, the better organized you are, the more efficient you'll be. You'll also save yourself a lot of stress by being able to locate what you need easily.

Some people like to have a peg board over their workbench to hang their tools on. This is a good idea as is to have a bulletin board so you can hang the plans for your current project.

Last, you'll need good lighting. You can get shop lights inexpensively at discount stores like Wal-Mart or Home Depot.

Now that you have a place to work, what do you need to get started? The obvious answer would be wood, which we'll talk about a little later. What's the second obvious answer? Tools!

BEGINNING TOOL BOX

If you plan to make woodworking a hobby for a long time, you're better off buying good tools instead of the cheaper one. They'll hold up better and last longer.

As far as hand tools, you'll be fine buying used older ones as long as they're in good condition. The quality of older tools tends to be better and they're made to last.

You can build quality projects with just hand tools, but power tools make the job so much easier. Be especially leery of buying used or discounted power tools. Make sure they are safe and work effectively.

You don't have to rush out and buy everything all at once. This is a hobby that can earn you money which can be used to buy tools and material, it may even turn into a livelihood if you are not careful!

When you get the word out to friends and family members that you are delving into woodworking, a lot of them may have excess tools lying around that you can use. Reward any kindness with a beautiful piece once you get started!

Following are the basic tools you'll need.

Claw hammers are the most common types of hammers used for woodworking and general repairs around the home. They are available with different types of handles, wood, steel with rubber or plastic grips and fiberglass composition. The style of hammer you select should be a personal decision, hold the hammer in your hand as if to strike a nail, it should feel balanced, the grip should be comfortable.

There are different weights, 16 ounces is a good general purpose choice, for heavier work perhaps 20 ounces.

Smaller weights are suitable for tacks and light work or children.

Screwdrivers are needed for almost every woodworking project. Make sure you have various sizes of both Phillips head and flat head screwdrivers. I'm especially partial to my cordless, electric screwdriver that comes with different size bits for all types of projects. This way, I have one tool with all the versatility of 10!

Wood chisels range in size from 1/4" to 2" wide in 1/8" graduations. They are available with wooden or plastic handles.

Use a chisel about one half the width of the cut to be made. Thin cuts can be made by pushing by hand; heavier cuts are made by tapping on the end with a wooden mallet. You'll want a couple of different sizes of chisels – no need to buy all sizes when you're just starting out!

Levels are available in many sizes and shapes, the most common being 24" long. They can be made of wood, aluminum or plastic. Some have fixed vials, others are adjustable. All levels have one or more vials for vertical and horizontal use, some have 45 degree vials. Inside the vial is a fluid with an air bubble, when the bubble is centered between the two indicator lines the surface is level. You'll need a level to insure your project turns out straight. You don't want to build a bookshelf only to see it listing at a 45 degree angle!

Framing Squares are important in woodworking. With this tool it is possible to layout and measure just about everything in the construction of a house from the basement stairs on up to the attic rafters. It may also be referred to as a steel square or a carpenter's square. The most common size has a 24" blade and a 16" tongue, however there are smaller sizes available but like some cheaper versions of the larger style they do not have the framing tables stamped on them.

Try Square - These squares have a steel tongue fixed into a wooden handle, they range in size from 3" to 12", some have inch scales on them others are blank. They are very handy for furniture and cabinet making as they are small enough to fit in confined spaces.

Triangles - These are available in many shapes and sizes in various materials, the double 45° and a 30° - 60° are the two shapes used most in laying out patterns.

Tape measures come in a variety of widths and lengths. I would not recommend anything less than 3/4" wide for a tape over 6 feet long as they can not be extended out and remain rigid. For small projects in the shop 1/2" wide ones are adequate. Some have highlighted indicators at each foot; others have them at 16 inch intervals which is handier in construction for stud layout, whereas the foot indicators are more useful in the shop. Special tapes are available for lefties as well as ones with digital read-outs. The hook on the end is meant to be loose so that it will give an accurate measurement whether it is hooked over the edge or butted up to an edge. Check if the hook has been bent if measurements are not accurate.

Nail and Screws – you can buy these as needed for various projects, but you should still keep on hand various sizes of nails and screws.

Sandpaper – You'll use a lot of sandpaper in finishing your projects. Have various grades available for the different projects you'll be completing. Fine grit paper is used for most wood projects. Medium is generally used for first sanding of soft woods and shaping. Coarse grit should be used for paint removal, rough sanding, and shaping.

Various Saws – A fret saw use very narrow blades so intricate designs can be cut. The blade can be rotated a full 360° to negotiate tight corners. Inside cuts are started by drilling a small hole to allow the blade to pass through it.

Then the blade is inserted into the saw frame. Deep throated saws called scroll saws with frames having 18" clearance are available. Handsaws are available in many sizes and configurations; a good general purpose saw is 26" long and has 8 teeth per inch. Crosscut saws (to cut across the grain) have teeth with a negative rake; ripping saws (to cut in the direction of the grain) have a zero rake.

Hand Plane - There are many different styles of hand planes some made of steel, others made from wood. Most are meant to smooth the surface, there are some with blades designed to cut profiles but with the advent of the router these are less common. Squaring up board edges and cleaning up rough boards is easy work with a hand plane. While you only need a basic smoothing plane to tackle most projects, don't buy the cheapest hand plane you find. Look for a brand name or at least good quality metal to be sure the plane will last a long time.

Clamps - Any project that is glued requires clamping to insure that the parts are bonded firmly in exactly the right position. You can never have too many clamps, it is a good idea to pick up any that are available for a good price, especially at swap meets and garage sales no matter what style they are.

You'll use clamps to glue boards side to side and to hold projects together as joints dry. Buying pipe clamps that range from 18 inches to 8 feet wide should ensure you have the right clamp for most projects. Add a few hand clamps and small C-clamps for smaller projects, too. If you intend to work with oak a lot, consider buying pipe clamps with zinc- coated pipes to prevent staining of the wood.

Vises – A vise holds wood pieces steady on the workbench as you shape them with other tools. A mid-size vise, with a 7- to 9-inch opening, is sufficient for a beginner. Look for a vise with wood jaws or inserts, or use smooth scrap wood to keep the vise from denting your projects.

Rasps - Rough metal rasps are used to file board edges and remove small amounts of wood. Two rasps, one fine and one coarse, should be all you need

Electric Drill and Drill Bits - Electric drills are by far the first power tool purchased, they have so many uses besides drilling holes, there are attachments to turn them into paint mixers, sanders, screwdrivers, saws, grinders, lathes, the list goes on.

There are corded and cordless drills, so far each have their place. I would recommend starting with a 3/8" capacity, variable speed, reversible corded drill, it will not be as handy as a cordless but you will get good performance for a low price.

Choose a slower speed model, (max. 1200 rpm), they seem to have more torque for drilling larger holes yet still drill clean smaller holes. Most drills are now double insulated which is a safety factor, if it has a three prong plug use a three prong extension cord.

Electric Circular Saw – These can be very handy when cutting your wood pieces. No need to break the bank on this, however. Find one that's easy for you to use and reliable.

Jig Saw – While not completely necessary, a good jig saw can help make your woodworking projects easier. They can add some eye-catching detail to a piece and make cutting wood easier as well.

Router - Routers have become one of the most used tools in a workshop, possibly even more popular than a table saw. A well equipped shop will have both a plunge base and a fixed base router; it is now possible to get a combination kit where one machine has both bases.

There are many different bit profiles available, probably a straight bit and a round over bit are the first ones you will need, but this depends on the type of projects you will be doing. It is much easier to work with smaller pieces if the router is mounted on a table. Generally much better results are achieved by taking several passes making a shallow cuts rather than one pass if a lot of material has to be removed.

Glue – You'll want some strong carpenter's wood glue on hand to insure your piece's stability.

Carpenter's Pencil - Rectangular shaped pencil, about 1/4" X 1/2", with a 1/16" X 3/16" lead.

Keep **safety glasses** at hand, even if you aren't using power tools in your wood shop. When using a hammer or moving boards, objects or wood shavings can fly up quickly, putting you at risk of injury.

A basic **first aid kit** should also be readily available for shop accidents, though you can greatly reduce your risk of wood shop accidents by always using your hand tools as they are intended. Using the right tool for the job saves wear and tear on the tools and on you.

Finally, keep a **wet / dry shop vacuum** nearby so that you can quickly clean up wood shavings and dust. Keeping dust and wood particles to a minimum will reduce the risk of wood shop fires and help you breathe easier, too.

We'll assume you have a basic knowledge in using a hammer and screwdriver. If you will be using power tools, just rely on the instruction guide that will come with it if you buy it new. If you don't buy it new, enlist the help of a family member or friend to show you. A last ditch resort is to check the Internet or get a book from your local library.

Using tools isn't rocket science. They're pretty easy to figure out if you take the time. Just remember to be careful and practice safe use.

What do you need to know about using mechanical tools? Read on!

TAKING CARE OF YOUR WOODWORKING TOOLS

Few things are more exciting than getting a new power tool! After saving the money, doing the research and all the comparative shopping, finally receiving the box and calling it your own is a great feeling.

Machines: they will cut, they will drill, and they will flatten or chop almost anything. But you have to take care of them. Read and understand the owner's manual, then keep it for later reference. Once a machine is set up, it still needs to be checked periodically for alignment, for bolts needing tightening, for lubrication and cleaning.

Learn to 'tune' each machine within its tolerances: band saw wheels need to run in the same plane, a drill press needs to raise and lower vertically square to its table, and a table saw blade must be ninety degrees square to its tabletop, with the front and rear of the blade running parallel to its miter slots. Books are a good source of information of this sort.

Before you load a motor with heavy use, allow it to build up to full force so it can do its job efficiently. New machines, especially, need to be allowed to run several minutes before heavy use a first time, to allow the brushes in the motor to 'seat.' Learn the sound of the motor on each machine, and pay attention to how it sounds under the load of an operation. If something's wrong, you'll often be able to hear or feel it from the machine before things go further a wry.

Don't try to work any machine too fast. If a procedure takes excessive force, something is probably amiss such as: hardened wood or not enough chip clearance for a blade, or misalignment of essential parts. If you feel the work is overtaxing the machine, find a different way to do it, or approach the job in smaller steps.

Know ahead of time where your 'panic button' is.

Practice holding the work- piece clear of the blade, then turning the machine on and off. Before you begin, know where that off-switch is, and know how you are going to get to it.

There are after-market aids to make off-buttons accessible by your knee rather than fumbling for it by hand.

Always unplug a machine when handling or changing blades. Not only can bumping a switch give you a nasty surprise, but faulty switches (even the 'safer' magnetic switches) have been known to connect and come on with a sudden blow to a tabletop, such as a dropped tool or piece of wood. If there is a power outage, unplug each machine individually and leave the lights on to tell you when the power has been restored.

Keep your machines clean. Vacuum the dust out of motor vents, off belts, switches, pulleys and inside router collets. Keep band saw tires clean with a toothbrush and isopropyl alcohol, turning the wheels by hand.

If you have a rack and pinion height adjustment, be sure its teeth and gears are kept free of sawdust buildup.

As a rule, see that your work piece is securely clamped in place or guided as it passes a blade. Never cut freehand on a table saw; stabilize the work piece against a fence or miter gauge, but don't use the two together because that may bind the work piece against the blade and cause a nasty kickback or jamming of the blade. A panel-cutting sled riding in the miter slot is the safest way to do cross-cuts.

With hand held power tools, before you begin, plan how the electrical cord will pass freely as you complete the operation, and if your cord is of adequate length (this is one great advantage of battery-operated tools.) Be certain a cord isn't going to snag on something unnecessarily or coil around your feet.

The best advice on new machinery is, educate yourself, and practice before you begin the work. Woodworking is wonderful hobby, but you are responsible for your own safety.

So now you're outfitted and have advice on your tools. Let's look at some woodworking terminology you might not be familiar with.

WOODWORKING GLOSSARY

- **Adhesive**

A substance that is capable of bonding material together by surface attachment.

- **Air Dried**

Lumber stacked and stored so that it is dried naturally by the exposure to air.

- **Allen Head**

A screw head with a recess requiring a hexagon shaped key, used mainly on machinery. These may be in metric or SAE sizes.

- **Apron**

This is a frame around the base of a table to which the top and legs are fastened.

- **Bench Dogs**

Pegs that go into holes in the top of a workbench which work with a vise to hold wide material.

- **Biscuit Joint**

An oval shaped disk that when inserted in a slot with glue swells to form a tight bond. A special tool is required to cut the slot.

- **Block Plane**

A small plane designed for cutting across end grain.

- **Board Foot**

Measurement of lumber equal to one square foot an inch thick or 144 cubic inches. Multiply width in inches X length in inches X thickness in inches, divide by 144 for total board feet.

- **Box Joint**

Square shaped finger joints used to join pieces at right angles.

- **Butt Joint**

A joint where the edges of two boards are against each other.

- **Caliper**

An instrument with two legs, one of them sliding, used to measure the thickness of objects.

- **Chuck**

An attachment to hold work or a tool in a machine, lathe chucks and drill chucks are examples.

- **Compound Miter**

An angled cut to both the edge and face of a board, most common use is with crown molding.

- **Cross Cut**

A cut which runs across the board perpendicular to the grain.

- **Dado**

A groove in the face of a board, usually to accept another board at 90 degrees as in shelf uprights.

- **Dovetail Joint**

A joint where the fingers are shaped like a doves tail, used to join pieces at 90 degrees.

- **Dowel**

A wood pin used to align and hold two adjoining pieces.

- **Dowel Center**

Metal buttons that go into a predrilled dowel hole to mark the position for drilling the second piece.

- **Epoxy Glue**

A two part glue that practically glues anything to anything, including metal to metal.

- **European Hinge**

A hidden style hinge fastened to the door with a cup hole.

- **Filler**

A substance that is used the fill pores and irregularities on the surface of material to decrease the porosity before applying a finishing coat.

- **Finger Joint**

Long tapered fingers used to join material lengthwise, often used in manufacturing molding to join short lengths.

- **Grain**

The appearance, size and direction of the alignment of the fibers of the wood.

- **Hand Plane**

A tool to smooth and true wood surfaces, consisting of a blade fastened in frame at an angle with hand grips to slide it along the board.

- **Jig**

A device used to hold work or act as a guide in manufacturing or assembly.

- **Joiner**

A machine used to true the edges of boards usually in preparation for gluing.

- **Kerf**

The width of a saw cut determined by the thickness and set of the blade.

- **Kick Back**

This is when a work piece is thrown back by a cutter, prevented using anti-kick back devices on power tools such as table saws.

- **MDF**

Medium density fiberboard, very stable underlay for counter tops etc. to be covered with laminate

- **Miter Box**

An apparatus to guide a saw to make miter joints.

- **Miter Gauge**

A guide with an adjustable head that fits in a slot and slides across a power tool table to cut material at an angle.

- **Miter Joint**

Pieces are cut on an angle to make a joint.

- **Molding (Moulding)**

A strip of material with a profile cut on the facing edges, used for trimming.

- **Ogee**

An S shape that is made by making one cut to produce two identical pieces.

- **Particle Board**

A generic term for material manufactured from wood particles and bound together with glue

- **Plumb**

A term used to describe something that is perfectly perpendicular to the earth relative to gravity. A plumb bob on the end of a string will give you a line that is plumb or straight up and down.

- **Plywood**

A glued wood panel usually 4' X 8' made up of thin layers of wood laid at right angles to each other.

- **Rip Cut**

A cut which runs through the length of a board parallel to the grain.

- **Sawhorse**

A trestle usually used in pairs to hold wood for cutting.

- **Spline**

A thin strip of wood fitted between two grooves to make a joint.

- **T - slot**

A slot milled in the shape of an upside down T to hold special bolts for clamps or jigs.

- **Table Saw**

A circular saw mounted under a table with height and angle adjustments for the blade.

- **Taper Cut**

A cut where the width decreases from one end to the other, these are usually done on a table saw with a jig.

- **Tear out**

The tendency to splinter the trailing edge of material when cutting across the grain.

- **Template**

A pattern to guide the marking or cutting of a shape, often a router is used with a piloted bit.

- **Tenon**

A projection made by cutting away the wood around it to insert into a mortise to make a joint.

- **Tongue and Groove**

A joinery method where a board has a protruding tongue on one edge and a groove on the other, the tongue of one board fits into the groove of the next.

- **Witness Marks**

These are marks put on boards or pieces to keep them in order during gluing, joining and assembly.

- **X-Acto Knife**

This is a razor like blade in a handle; the blades come in various shapes, very handy for fine work.

There are so many different terms used in woodworking. The above is certainly only a partial list. You will find yourself learning the terminology as you become more and more familiar with the world of carpentry and woodworking.

When you enter into the world of woodworking, there's one thing you simply cannot do without – wood!

PICKING OUT YOUR WOOD

The two basic categories of wood are hardwood and softwood. There is also manufactured wood like plywood.

What you use for any given project depends on various factors: strength, hardness, grain characteristics, cost, stability, weight, color, durability and availability. Usually beginning woodworkers start out with softwood such as pine. It's soft and easy to work, and you don't need expensive tools to get good results. It is readily available at local lumberyards and home centers. It has it's limitations in furniture making; it is a soft wood and will damage easily.

Softwood is from an evergreen or coniferous (cone-bearing) tree. Common varieties are pine, fir, spruce, hemlock, cedar and redwood. These woods are mostly used in the home construction industry. Cedar and redwood are excellent choices for outdoor projects, while pine is often used for "Early American Country Style" furniture.

Pine and most other softwoods will absorb and lose moisture more than hardwoods so are not as stable.

Purchase the lumber at least two weeks before starting your project and keep it indoors.

You will find that softwoods are sold in standard thickness and widths, for example a 1 X 4 will be 3/4" thick and 3 1/2" wide similar to construction materials. The material will usually be priced per lineal foot and the price will increase accordingly for the wider boards.

Hardwood lumber comes from deciduous trees, the ones that shed their leaves annually. Popular domestic species are oak, maple, cherry, birch, walnut, ash and poplar. Of these common native hardwoods, only red oak and poplar are usually stocked in home centers and lumberyards, the others have to be obtained from specialty stores. The material stocked at home centers and lumberyards is usually sold in similar dimensions to softwood and by the lineal foot as well.

At specialty stores the thickness of hardwood lumber is specified in quarters of an inch, measured when the wood is in a rough state. The thinnest stock is 4/4, representing 1 in., and the thickest usually available is 16/4, representing 4 in. Rather than being milled to specified dimensions, like pine, hardwoods are sold in random widths and lengths.

Working with hardwoods is quite different from working with pine; you cannot drive a screw through hardwood lumber without first boring a pilot hole. Cutting and planing hardwoods requires extremely sharp tools.

Hardwoods are good to use when building furniture.

Oak and ash are known as open-grain woods. These species have alternating areas of relatively porous and dense wood, when stained the open-grain areas absorb the color readily while the harder areas are more resistant. This accentuates the grain patterns, creating a dramatic effect.

Cherry, maple and birch are closed-grain woods, demonstrating a more uniform texture throughout a board. Poplar is also a closed-grain wood, but its color ranges from a beige to olive green, and often has purple highlights thrown into the mix. Because of this unusual coloration, it is rarely used if a furniture piece is going to have a clear finish. This wood is best when stained or even painted. Poplar, being less expensive, is also a good choice for framing hardwood projects.

Hardwood is more durable and less prone to dents and scratches. It is also more expensive but will finish to a better advantage. Soft woods, like pine, are more prone to dents and scratches and do not have the durability of hardwood.

Softwoods are much less expensive and easier to find. Ask your lumber supplier to show you "Class 1" or "Select Grade" lumber. Make sure it is properly dried, straight, and free of knots and defects. (It may be impossible to be completely free of defects but be sure you understand how to cut around these.)

The two most common manufactured sheets goods used in furniture making are MDF (Medium Density Fiberboard) and Particle Board. Both are made from wood particles, combined with glue and bonded under pressure. MDF has finer particles than Particle Board so produces a smoother and stronger finished product.

MDF machines very well and is often used for moulded components on painted furniture. Its main draw back is that it is a very heavy product compared to real wood.

Because of their laminated construction, they are extremely stable in all dimensions. Since the veneers on any given panel are usually cut sequentially from the same log, the panel should display a uniform color and grain. Matching the grain pattern of solid wood to the generally uniform grain pattern on the panels can be difficult. But careful planning can yield good matches in the most visible areas of your project.

Manufactured sheets do have limitations, whenever they are used, regardless of the core, the edge must be hidden and the veneers on the surface are extremely thin, often less than 1/32 in. Because of this, the surface is fragile and has a tendency to split out, especially on the back side of a saw cut. Also, since the veneer is so thin aggressive sanding can quickly work through the veneer and expose the unattractive core underneath.

As we said, what wood you use depends on what kind of project you are undertaking. For projects that will be painted, you can use simply MVF. For furniture, it's often a good idea to choose something that will finish well like cedar or oak.

You'll most likely be getting your wood from a lumber supply store or a home improvement store like Home Depot or Lowe's. There are a few things you need to keep in mind when picking out your lumber.

At the lumber yard or store, you'll find wood boards stacked up in high piles according to length, quality grade, thickness, wood type and many other categories. Even in piles of boards that are grouped as being the same, there are differences in quality, so follow these simple tips for choosing boards that will work for your woodworking projects.

Don't take boards you don't want! Lumberyard novices may feel like they have to take the boards that are first presented to them. Don't be afraid to examine each board closely and send boards back if they don't meet your criteria. Why pay for a warped board that won't work in your current project? Rejecting boards is not an insult, but a way to pay for wood you can use, so get in the habit early.

Check for straightness. Hold the board at eye level on one end, with the other end on the ground. Look down the board to see if it has obvious curves or twists. Some projects can handle a curved board, but for beginners, working with curved boards may be too complicated.

Check for splits and warping. Look over both sides of the board to see if there are any long splits or warped edges. Splits and warps reduce the amount of wood you can use for your project, so pass on boards that would result in a lot of waste.

Knotholes can be considered attractive in some kinds of woodworking projects, so if you're looking for a really knotty piece of wood, that's fine. Otherwise, check your boards for large knotholes that would become waste wood or loose knot pieces that may fall out, causing gaps or weak areas in your cut pieces.

For fine woodworking projects or projects that need a straight, even grain, quarter sawn lumber offers even wood graining, but is more expensive than regular plain sawn lumber.

Decide whether you're willing to pay for the straight grain before choosing boards.

Look closely at each board to see if the color is even enough for your project, and that there are not a large number of wormholes or other marred areas. Also check for lumberyard chalk or pen markings or dents that may not come off easily.

Used boards gathered from old barns or other projects can be interesting and fun to work with. However, when buying or choosing reclaimed lumber, check for signs of decay. If the board is spongy or soft, or has signs of fungus on it, it may not hold up well as project wood.

Pressure-treated lumber and chemically treated lumber are for use in outdoor projects, and are better able to withstand temperature and moisture changes. If you're building a deck or outdoor project, ask for treated lumber.

Otherwise, untreated boards are a better choice.

The beginning woodworker should probably start out using softer woods like pine or spruce. They are easier to work, and you can eventually move up to harder woods like oak and cedar.

You're almost ready to get started, but first let's review some safety procedures all good woodworkers adhere to.

SAFETY IN THE SHOP

When you are working around sharp saws, machinery that can sever a limb, and heavy boards, it's important to be safe and avoid any mistakes that could endanger your health and even your life!

Safety glasses or goggles should be worn whenever power tools are in use and when chiseling, sanding, scraping or hammering overhead. This is very important for anyone wearing contact lenses. Wear ear protectors when using noisy power tools. Some tools operate at noise levels that damage hearing.

Be careful of loose hair and clothing so that it does not get caught in tools; roll your sleeves up and remove jewelry. Keep tools out of the reach of small children.

The proper respirator or face mask should be worn when sanding, sawing or using substances with toxic fumes. Oily rags are spontaneously combustible, so take care when you store and discard them.

Keep blades sharp. A dull blade requires excessive force and can slip which causes accidents.

Always use the right tool for the job. Repair or discard tools with cracks in the wooden handles or chips in the metal parts.

Don't drill, shape or saw anything that isn't firmly secured. Don't abuse your tools.

Do not work with tools when you are tired. That's when most accidents occur. Do not work with tools when you have been using alcohol. Alcohol can skew your judgment. Wait to celebrate after you've finished your project! Do not smoke around flammable product like stains and solvents.

Read the owner's manual for all tools and under- stand their proper usage. Unplug all power tools when changing settings or parts.

Take special care regarding the use of the table saw fence settings and the suggestions on how to make cuts using safety guards, push sticks, push blocks, fence straddlers, and feather boards.

The most powerful tool in your shop is your brain, use it. Thinking your cuts and movements through before acting can help save both fingers and scrap wood. Pay attention to your actions. Looking up to watch the shop TV or visitor can result in your hand contacting the blade. Always wait until you have completed your cut before you take your eyes off the blade.

Keep in mind that this is just a hobby and take a break when you feel rushed or frustrated with a project. Mistakes happen when we rush to complete a job. If your saw is resisting the cut, stop and see what's wrong. A misaligned rip fence or improperly seated throat plate can sometimes cause a board to get stuck in mid cut. Forcing the board in these situations may cause kickback or contact with the blade. Take a moment to evaluate the situation and determine the problem.

Let the tool stop running. Giving the power tool time to wind down after a cut is an often-overlooked safety mistake. Even without power, the spinning blade can still do a lot of damage.

Accidents are caused by inattention, taking chances, bad judgment, fatigue, and horseplay. Other causes are poor instruction (not reading manuals), missing guards, unsuitable clothing, defective equipment, insufficient working space and poor lighting.

A huge step in preventing personal injury is to familiarize yourself with any new tool before using it, read the manual, do a dry run with the machine unplugged. Only use a tool or machine for its intended purpose.

If it is a two person job don't try to do it alone, wait until assistance is available.

Keep a clean shop. A cluttered shop is an accident waiting to happen. Keeping your shop clean will help protect you, and your tools, from tripping hazards. Designate where hand tools are stored, sort nails, screws, and other hardware in containers. Sweep up at the end of the day. Solvent fumes and airborne dust can present health and explosion hazards. Care should be taken to ensure a supply of fresh air and use only explosion proof vent fans.

Just as there are safety procedures you should follow, it helps if you are aware of the most common mistakes newbies make when beginning their wood projects.

COMMON MISTAKES

The single most common mistake in any do it yourself project is the failure to read and follow the manufacturer's instructions for any tool or material being used. Other common mistakes include taking the safety measures that are laid out for a project for granted and poor project planning. Here is a list of hints to successfully complete this project and to do it safely.

Follow the "Golden Rule" of measuring: "Measure twice, cut once." And provide yourself plenty of time for each step.

Understand your plan. Whether it's a pre-made plan you purchased or downloaded, be sure you know the steps you have to take to finish the project. Don't be too stringent, however. Be willing to alter your plans if needed to finish the piece in a way that's easiest for you.

Do not neglect your tools and machinery. Make sure you take care of them with cleaning and maintenance on a regular basis. Ensure that metal surfaces are free of rust and blades are kept sharp.

Use a sharp pencil or marking knife to make layout marks on your wood. You must be able to see your markings in order to complete the piece correctly.

Use the same tape measure throughout your whole project. Unfortunately, tape measures aren't manufactured to be precision measuring devices. The hook on the end slides to compensate for its own thickness when changing between hooking it on the outside of something being measured and pushing it against the interior of something for an interior measurement. Avoid using the hook on the end. Try to start at the one inch mark, but remember to subtract that extra inch for the correct measurement.

The second and most important thing is to use the same tape measure for every measurement in the project. This will cancel out the variations between tapes. And if you do use the hook, use it for ALL the measurements.

Don't cut all the parts out at once and expect to have an assembling party with the pieces. This is a common newbie mistake and should be avoided. Why? The first reason is that there could be mistakes in the pattern or plan. If you cut out all of the parts first, and there is more than one mistake, you will

49

have several good quality bits of firewood at your disposal for winter! It is better to do things in stages and learn that the plan is riddled with mistakes first.

The second problem is with wood movement. Changes in humidity and temperature can cause the wood to warp after being cut. This will affect all of your joinery. The best way to counteract this is to break the project down into stages.

The next section will look at some basic joints to join pieces of wood together.

JOINTS

You can have a more finished and professional look to your work by using joints instead of screws and nails. Here are some of the basic joints used in woodworking.

Butt Joints

The butt joint is the simplest of the woodworking joints, and is very easy for beginners to master. The joint consists of two board ends that are pushed, or butted, together and held with nails, screws or glue. Simple wood boxes are often constructed with butt joints. While the butt joint offers a quick finish, it does not offer structural strength in most cases. If a butt joint held together with nails is required to bear much weight, the nails may soon pull out of the wood.

For beginners, though, the butt joint offers an easy way to complete a project without expensive equipment or in-depth woodworking knowledge.

Dowel Joints

This technique is ideal for joining two flat pieces together to form a larger flat surface.

Take two pieces of equal length wood. Decide now which side will be the top and which the bottom for each piece and mark the top side of each so that you do not forget.

Clamp both pieces together, one on top of the other, with the bottoms face to face in the middle. When clamping, ensure that the two surfaces along which you plan to join these pieces of wood are level with each other (see diagram one).

Draw a line down the middle of each surface to be joined. This must be exactly the same on both pieces of wood, otherwise when they are joined there will be a step at the join. Once this line has been drawn, use a set square and mark lines across the grain of the wood. The intersection of the length and width lines will show where the dowel holes will be drawn.

There is no hard and fast rule for how many dowels should be used. However, the heavier the weight of whatever will be on the surface, the more dowels should be used. Typically, one dowel per foot is a good rule (with a minimum of two).

Once these lines have been drawn you can then proceed to drill the holes at the marked intersections. The drill bit used should match the diameter of the dowel being used, thus ensuring a tight fit.

As for the dowel itself, you can either make your own small dowels from a longer length, or you can buy dowel made specifically for this reason. The latter option is a far better solution, as the small dowels are beveled at the ends to make it easier to but them in the holes, and are ribbed to allow the glue to bond more efficiently. Each hole should be just over half as deep as the length of the dowel being used.

Once the holes have been drilled, glue one end of each dowel into the holes in the first piece of wood. Then place glue along the full length of the second piece, ensuring that some glue falls into each of the holes.

Unclamp the two pieces and push them together, ensuring that the two top markings are facing up. Once done you should clamp tightly overnight. Be careful when you clamp them to make sure that both pieces remain flat and do not try and warp upwards. To avoid this, it may be necessary to clamp the entire piece down to a flat surface.

Dovetail Joints

The dovetail joint is possibly the best joint that you can use to join two pieces of wood together at a right angle. Not only is it a very strong joint, but it also adds to the appeal of the woodworking project.

The simplest way to create dovetail joints is to use a router and a dovetail template jig. The latter is available from any good home improvement store and can cost as little as $70. It's well worth the investment if you plan on doing many dovetail joints in the future.

Arrange the three pieces of the drawer or box as shown in the first diagram and mark the inside and outside of each piece. In addition, mark the ends of each piece as it is imperative that when cutting the dovetails the correct two ends are cut at one go.

Clamp the front of the drawer and one side into the dovetail machine as follows: the left side of the drawer should be clamped under the front clamp (pointing upwards towards the template) with the inside of the drawer pointing out; the front of the drawer - again with the inside pointing out -should be clamped under the top clamp so that it butts up against the left drawer.

These two pieces should be staggered slightly, rather than being aligned exactly. The precise measurement will depend upon the particular dovetail machine that you are using, and this distance will be supplied with its manual.

However, it should be roughly in the region of 7/16 inch.

Once everything is tightly clamped in place, use the router to cut around the template, following the direction of the arrows in this diagram.

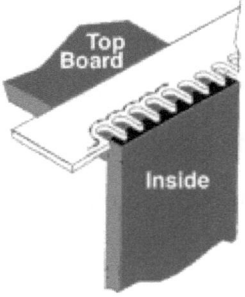

You can then join the boards together at the joints securing with glue and clamping overnight.

It is well worth practicing with scrap wood before trying the above procedure on any project as it will take a while to get the exact measurements (such as the depth of the router cut) perfect.

If the joint is too loose, slightly increase the depth of the router cut. If the joint is too tight (remember that you still have to squeeze some glue into the joint), slightly decrease the depth of the cut.

Slotted Tenon Joints

Slotted tenon joints are typically used as a method of fixing shelving into a unit's shelf walls. However, it can also be used for a number of other purposes.

The idea of a slotted tenon joint is that only one of the two pieces of wood needs to be modified in order to attain a good, tight fit. To do this, one piece has a slot made into it that is the same width as the thickness of the second piece of wood. This latter piece of wood can then be pushed into the groove, making a strong, right-angled join.

The most effective way of creating the groove (or slot) is to use a router. Although a chisel can be used, the quality of finish will not be the same (and it takes far longer to make).

Be careful when making the slot to ensure that it is not too wide, otherwise the joint will not be tight enough to work. It is far better to start with too tight a groove and then widen it.

A router is not always the best tool to use however. If the groove is to hold a piece of 1/4 inch (or smaller) plywood, you should use a circular saw instead, changing the depth of cut to as little as 1/4 inch. This smaller cut is ideal when making the joint for a back panel of a cabinet, such as a bedside cabinet.

Now that you have some basic information, let's get started with that first project!

BEGINNING YOUR JOURNEY

A good place to begin is to identify the kind of wood project you would like to attempt. It could be as simple and useful as a cutting board with an original shape, or a birdhouse, or a candleholder for the mantle, or a child's toy.

You can find ideas everywhere for woodworking projects. Perhaps you want to increase the amount of storage in your home with a simple cabinet. Maybe your child's toys are just everywhere and you want a toy box to store them in. The possibilities are endless!

Get ideas online. Buy woodworking magazines and check out the projects they have. Get inspired by things you see at craft fairs and flea markets. Try to reproduce that antique telephone stand you saw. Just don't try to take on anything too complicated or else you're liable to become frustrated and quit before you even get started.

As a beginning woodworker, you should choose an easy project. Putting together an armoire might not be the best starting project. Here are the plans for an easy magazine rack.

A MAGAZINE RACK

Building a magazine rack is a relatively easy project that you can complete in a weekend. It doesn't require much wood so you may even be able to make it out of the odds and ends lying around in your workshop.

Construction

Tools required: sander, router

Wood required:

Description	Qty	Width	Thickness	Length
Legs	4	2 1/4" (57 mm)	3/4" (19 mm)	15" (381 mm)
Top supports	2	2" (51 mm)	1/2" (13 mm)	16 1/2" (419 mm)
Center top support	1	1 1/2" (38 mm)	1/2" (13 mm)	19 1/4" (489 mm)
Center bottom support	1	1 1/2" (38 mm)	1/2" (13 mm)	16" (406 mm)
Bottom Supports	2	2" (51 mm)	1/2" (13 mm)	19 1/4" (489 mm)
Side edging	4	3/4" (19 mm)	1/4" (6 mm)	6 1/4" (159 mm)
Sides (plywood)	2	6 3/4" (171 mm)	1/2" (13 mm)	9" (229 mm)
Base (plywood)	1	7" (178 mm)	1/2" (13 mm)	16" (406 mm)

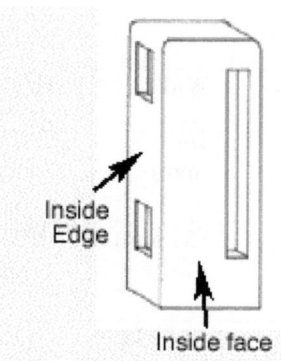

Inside
Edge

Inside face

The best place to begin this project is with the four leg pieces. Take one of the four legs are make the following routs in it:

1. On the inside (3/4") edge, make a rout that is 1/4" deep and 1/2" wide that runs from 1/2" from the top of the leg to 2 1/2" from the top. This rout should be 1/8" in from each side. This slot will accommodate the top support that runs along the length of the rack.

2. On the same side as step one, make a rout that is 1/4" deep and 1/2" wide that runs from 4" from the bottom of the leg to 6" from the bottom. Again, this rout should be 1/8" in from each side and it will accommodate the bottom support.

3. On the wide inside (2 1/4") face, make a rout that is 1/2" wide, 1/4" deep and that runs from 4 3/4" from the bottom to 13 3/4" from the bottom. The rout should be 1/2" in from the

outside edge of the leg (i.e. the edge that did not have routs 1 and 2 put into them).

Once you have made all of these routs, square off the rounded corners so that the sides, bottom and top slot tightly into them. Sand the leg rounding off the edges to give a softer look to the project. Then, repeat the above steps for the other three legs.

Before making the routs, make sure you have marked out the correct sides so that the inside edges all match up (i.e. face each other so that the top and bottom supports can be slotted in).

Next we need to make the slots in the bottom supports that will accommodate the base plywood. Cut a slot on the inside face (2") that is 1/4" deep and 1/2" wide. This slot should begin 1/2" from the lower edge and should be 16" long (therefore it should begin 1 5/8" from either end of the piece. Repeat this for the second of the bottom supports, squaring off the rounded ends of the slot to allow the base to fit in tightly.

Now construct one side, gluing the bottom and top supports into two of the legs to build on complete side. Then construct the second side by repeating this step. Once the glue is dry, connect these front and back constructions to the plywood sides and the base, again gluing them together.

You now have the main shape of the magazine rack completed. Glue the thin side edging pieces to the top and bottom of the plywood sides, thus hiding the plywood's edging. Now cut the center top support to the correct shape by cutting out a block from each end, as shown in this diagram.

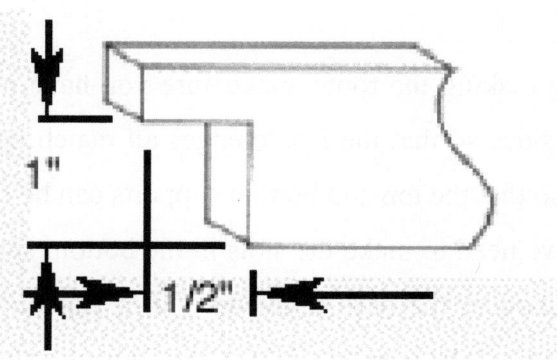

Once cut to shape, sand the piece to round off the edges and then glue it on top of the two plywood sides, half way between the front and back.

Finally, sand off the center bottom support and then glue into place on the plywood base, again half way between the front and back support (and therefore matching the position of the top center support).

Give the entire unit a thorough sanding and then stain and wax.

NOTE: If you don't have a router, you can still put together this piece using screws and putty for fill. Make sure you label the pieces and assemble according to the picture using butt joints.

Let's look at another good beginning piece of furniture.

STORAGE CHEST

This chest was designed to have a dual purpose: firstly (and most obviously) as a storage unit and secondly as a coffee table in a small living room. The shape is very basic, but is the most functional for storing toys and games in.

In order to improve the aesthetic appeal of the chest dovetail joints would be used to join the sides. Details of how to create easy dovetail joints has been included in the Joints section. However, it is not necessary to use dovetail joints: any form of jointing, such as dowel joints or butt joints could be used.

Construction: The base unit

The sides of the base piece were made out of pine with the front and back being of dimensions 30 x 9 x 3/4 inches and the sides 16 x 9 x 3/4.

Having cut these pieces to size, the first job is to create the dovetail joints. These are done using a router and a dovetail template (see joints section for more details) with the dovetail showing on the side pieces, not on the front and back.

Once the dovetails have been cut, the next job is to create a means of attaching the base wood into the front and sides. The base was made out of a piece of 1/2 inch thick plywood. To attach the base plywood to the sides and front, a slotted tenon joint was cut 1/2 inch from the bottom of the sides, back and front. The size of this slot is 1/2 inch wide (the same as the thickness of the plywood) and 3/8 inch deep.

The size of the base plywood is 29 1/2 inches long by approximately 16 inches wide. It is important that you take your own precise measurement of this piece once you have cut the dovetails as the exact dimensions will depend on the depth of the joint and so on. To measure this size, dry fit the four sides together and measure the dimensions of the inside of the box.

Then add on a measurement of 3/8 inch at each end for the depth of the slotted tenon joint.

When you have cut the base to size, glue the four sides and the base together and clamp for several hours, ensuring that the sides are at 90 degree angles to the front and back pieces.

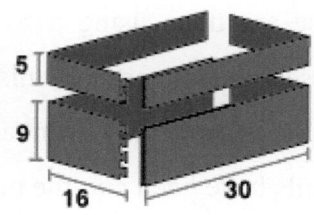

The lid

The lid is built in a very similar way. Cut out the front and back to the dimensions 30 x 5 x 3/4 inch, and the sides 16 x 5 x 3/4 inch and route out the dovetails. Take a moment to ensure that you are cutting the dovetails out of the sides (as you did on the base unit) rather than the front and back.

Unlike the base unit, you do not need to route out a slot for the lid. Instead, the lid is made from pine, of rough dimensions 30 x 16 x 3/4 inches. Again, take your own measurement by dry fitting the four sides. Obviously, to make a piece that is 16 inches wide, you will need to join two pieces of pine together by doweling them.

Glue the four sides together and then glue the top on. There is no need for screws or nails simply use strong wood glue and leave the whole unit clamped over night.

Finishing the project

Sand the entire chest, taking extra care to make sure that all of the corners are neatly rounded off - the last thing you want is sharp corners that you may bang your leg into - and then wax it.

Add two hinges to the back of the unit and a clasp to the front. In this project it is worth buying ornamental hinges and a clasp as it adds to the design - hiding the hinges will make the chest look rather dull.

Finally, add a chain or similar mechanism to the inside of the chest to stop the lid from swinging open too far, and consequently damaging the hinges.

If you will be using this for a toy box, please use non-latching hinges to avoid any accidents. They make bounce back hinges that are available at most hardware stores which are best for toy boxes.

Another great, easy woodworking project will bring joy to your yard. Let's look at the plans for an easy bird feeder.

A BIRDFEEDER

This particular feeder is designed to take bird seed, rather than the more typical left-over food scraps. The advantage of this style is that it can be filled up infrequently as it can store several weeks' worth of food at a time. The bird feeder is made out of pine and is stained to suit its locale. You can also paint it to fit your style and taste.

Construction

Tools required: jigsaw, drill Wood list (Pine):

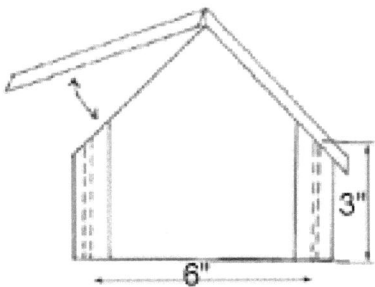

Description	Qty	Depth	Width	Length
Sides	2	3/4"	6"	6"
Roof parts	2	3/4"	5 1/2"	7"
Base	1	3/4"	8"	12"
Corner pieces	4 (dowel)	3/4"	3/4"	4"
Pole Stoppers	2	3/4"	3"	3"
Pole	1 (dowel)	1 1/2"	1 1/2"	6'
Plastic glass	2	1/8"	2 7/8"	6"
Hinges	2	1/2" deep		

First, the four corner pieces must have a quarter of the length cut out. The easiest way to do this is to clamp the corner piece in a vise and saw along the length until the saw cut is half way through the pole. Then rotate the corner piece by 90 degrees, re-clamp, and then cut through again until the waste quarter is loose. Repeat this procedure for all four corner pieces.

Glue a corner piece to each end of the side piece, ensuring that the base of the corner piece is aligned with the base of the side piece. However, there must be a thin gap between the corner piece and the end of the side piece that will allow the plastic glass to slot in (see diagram).

Once this is dry cut the side pieces to the correct shape for the roof. The roof should be at a 45 degree incline, reaching to a point in the middle.

Now cut the roof pieces to the required size. The apex of the roof should be angled by 45 degrees so that the two roof pieces rest snugly against each other. Then attach two small hinges between the two rood pieces (cutting a small slot so that the hinges do not cause a large gap between the roof pieces).

Cut the base piece to the desired shape. An irregular shape works well rather than trying to cut a geometrically- pleasing shape. Cut a hole in the middle of the base piece that is just large enough to accept the main pole.

Now it is time to fasten everything together. Slot the plastic glass into each end of the side pieces and attach this four-walled construction to the base by screwing up from the underside of the base (two screws in each side piece should be adequate). Then rest the roof on top of this construction, and screw one side of the roof into the side pieces. The other roof side is obviously not attached as this should hinge up to allow for the bird food to be added.

Then, wedge small pieces of wood into the base of the gap along which the plastic glass slides. This is done to create a gap between the base and the plastic glass, through which the bird food will spill out onto the base.

Finally, stain the wood to the desired color and varnish.

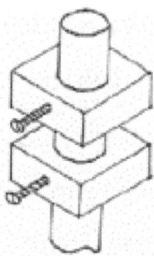

As said before, you can also paint the feeder to your own style.

To attach the main pole, make a hole in the pole stoppers that is just large enough to accept the pole. Then place one pole stopper on each side of the base hole, and pass the main pole through these three pieces. Screw through each pole stopper into the main pole and this adequately fix the pole to the base (see diagram).

We promised you a plan to make a workbench for your shop. This next plan is for just that.

A WORKBENCH

This workbench is simple to build and solid so it won't move around as you work on it. It is also small enough to fit in most workshops.

You'll need:

Part	Item	Dimensions
A	Top	198 x 48 x 1800mm
B	Corner brackets	90 x 35 x 240mm
C	Side top rails	148 x 48 x 800mm
D	Front/back top rails	90 x 35 x 1400mm
E	Coach bolts, nuts	
	and washers	5/16 x 4 ½
		5/16 x 6 ½
F	Side bottom rails	90 x 35 x 800mm
G	Legs	98 x 98 x 900mm
H	Front/back bottom	
	rails	90 x 35 x 1400mm
I	Shelf	800 x 1470 x 19mm
J	Bench stop	90 x 35 x 300mm

Tools

Claw hammer (570g) Smoothing plane (no. 4) Marking gauge Combination square Steel tape (3 meters)

Three beveled-edge firmer chisels (10mm, 18mm, 32mm) Cross-cut saw (650mm long)

Tenon saw (300mm long)

Nail punch (3mm) Set of twist drills

Set of screwdrivers (slotted, pozi, Phillips) Oil stone

Sanding cork

Variable-speed power drill Jigsaw

Circular saw

Here's how:

1. Cut to length the four legs (G) and mark in housings for top and bottom rails (D and H). The top housing is 148mm x 48mm deep; the lower one 90mm x 35mm deep. Set your circular saw to the right depth and cut on the waste side of the lines you marked. Cut a series of parallel lines about 12mm apart between the housing marks and knock out waste. Smooth each housing with a chisel or rasp.

2. Cut to length front and back top and bottom rails (D and H), align them in their housing and pin in place with nails. Drill through both legs and rails as shown and bolt rails to legs. Check frame is square by measuring the diagonals.

3. Cut and clamp side rails (C and F) to the front and back frame, then drill and insert the longer bolts. Tighten all nuts securely and check the table doesn't rock.

4. Cut out four corner brackets (B) with 45-degree angles. A miter saw will be useful for this or set a circular saw to cut at 45 degrees. Screw brackets in place flush with top of rails. At this stage the bench frame should be completely rigid.

5. Cut the bottom shelf (I) to suit the dimensions of the bench. Notch out 35mm x 133mm in each corner to clear the legs. The shelf can be screwed in place or left loose.

6. Cut the five pieces for the top (A). Move them around to get a good fit for the edges and hold them in place with a nail. Screw them to the bench frame with 100mm screws, two in each end, sunk slightly below the surface. Use a plane to smooth any major irregularities.

7. Prepare a bench stop (J) as shown in the detail. Find the center and measure 60mm and 200mm from one end of a length of 90mm x 35mm pine. Drill an 8mm diameter hole at these points. Draw two lines joining the holes and cut along lines with a jigsaw to form a slot. Smooth the cut with a file or sharp chisel. Bevel the end at 45 degrees. Cut bench to a length of 300mm.

8. Locate the bench stop where you want it. Right-handed people generally prefer the stop at the left-hand end of the bench and left-handed people vice-versa. Make sure you avoid the braces. Hold the bench stop against the front rails and mark around it on the underside of the bench top. Transfer this shape to the top of the bench.

Drill two holes in opposite corners and cut out the rectangular hole. Insert the bench stop and make sure it slides smoothly. Adjust with a file or chisel as necessary. Hold the bench stop so it is flush with the bench top and drill a hole through the front rail at the top of the slot. Insert a carriage bolt with a washer and wing nut to allow the bench stop to be raised and lowered easily.

9. Workbenches are usually not finished with paint or a clear finish as it could mark other items which are built on the bench.

Finally, let's look at a plan for some simple shelving units that can be put together in no time!

SHELVING

This is probably the most common woodworking project that people want to build. Who can't use more storage?

The best part about this project is that you can use standard size wood (2 x 3's) for the main framework and it can be put together without using complicated joinery.

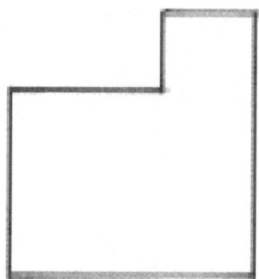

Construction

Tools required: Jigsaw, sander, drill

Wood required:

Description	Qty	Thickness	Length	Width
Main legs (2x3)	6	1 1/2"	72"	2 1/2"
Front and back supports	10	1 1/2"	96"	2 1/2"
Side supports	10	1 1/2"	15"	2 1/2"
Shelves (plywood)	5	1/2"	18"	98"

The first step is to prepare the front, back and side supports. These pieces need to have a 1/2" deep slot routed out of them that is 1" wide (see diagram). The shelves will fit into these slots, thus giving a nice finishes look to the shelving rather than showing the edge of the plywood.

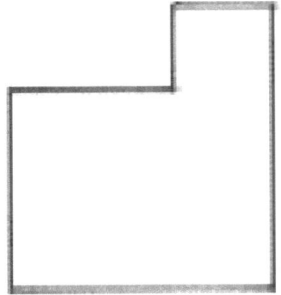

Once you have cut out all of the slots, it is time to construct the two side frameworks. To construct a side frame, take two of the leg supports and lay them flat on the floor so that the 2 1/2" width is showing. Then, attach the side supports (with the routed groove pointing up and inwards) by gluing and screwing through the 2 1/2" width (see diagram).

Ideally, the side supports should be attached at even intervals (every 30"), but you can modify this to suit your own requirements. Repeat for the other side, taking care to ensure that the routed groove points towards the middle of the shelving unit. Take the time to ensure that all joints are square; otherwise you may end up with a shelving unit that leans!

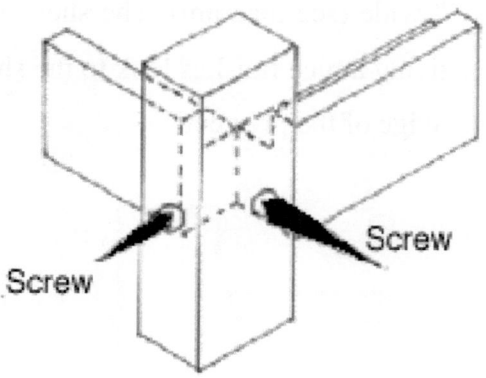

Once the sides are complete (and the glue has dried) it is time to attach the front and back supports. Again, these are attached using glue and screws, and should match the heights of the side pieces. Once attached, the result should be a complete frame. To strengthen this frame, take one of the two remaining leg pieces and attach it in the middle of the front frame by simply gluing and screwing into the support pieces. This will stop the unit from sagging in the middle.

Take the shelving pieces (which should be cut to shape as mentioned in the wood list) and cut a small notch out of the corner of each one. This notch should be a 1" by 1" square and will allow the shelves to sit snuggly against the four corner legs. Now, place the shelves into place. To do this, slide them in from the back (the front central leg makes it impossible from the front).

Once all shelves are in place, and everything looks okay, attach the final leg to the center of the back frame (thus matching the front one). Sand the unit thoroughly and paint if so desired.

Now that you've got a couple of projects to start with, we think it's important for you to realize that not everything has to be "cookie cutter" designed. There are times when you need to improvise.

WHAT IF SOMETHING GOES WRONG

One of the first hurdles a new woodworker must get past is the fear of messing up a project, and one of the best ways to tackle that apprehension is to simply "think outside the box". Most beginners decide to start with something simple (but may not know which projects have simple joinery) and then set out on a search for preprinted plans to make such- and-such.

It can become frustrating if personal help is not available. There are several ways to cure this, but here is one that has worked for many: forget other people's plans. Design what you need yourself. It isn't as hard as one might think, because there are always some kinds of limiting parameters to start with.

A bookshelf must be 10" deep so the books will slide into it, and shelf spacing will match the height of your tallest books, plus one inch for finger room. A curio shelf will be sized by the space available to accommodate it, or by the objects to be displayed on it. Bed frames should fit standard mattress sizes, and doors…well, there are your openings to measure.

The point is, don't be afraid to begin these projects on your own. There is a vast knowledge base of woodworking advice available in printed matter and online. If the project doesn't turn out as you'd planned, you can always start over, and you will have learned a great deal along the way. We often learn more from our mistakes in working wood than from easy successes.

Why not try to design your own piece? Drawing ideas out freehand on paper is helpful. What if it were this way, or that way? Hand sketches will show you how ideas can come together, or clash with each other. Then, if you know the shelf must fit a space five feet high overall, the number of shelves to include will be dictated by the height of the items to be stored. Heavy or larger items (or spaces) usually go near the bottom of a unit, to anchor it physically as well as to the eye when viewed from across a room. Spaces can also be broken up and not continuous across the entire front.

Designs can also be planned based on what wood a woodworker may have available. If you have several 2x4s sitting around, an Early American or pinewood look may be called for. Be certain to carefully square up any stock.

Construction castoffs are easily ripped to usable dimensions on a table saw, but learn the safety procedures for your machine before trying to rip long boards.

Designing your own project can also mean adapting someone else's plan to your own use. It's quite common for a woodworker to see the ideal blanket chest, sofa table or display case, and then think "But I want mine to be..." and redesign the entire structure. Don't be afraid to trust your instincts and be innovative in making a piece. Educate yourself; ask questions of others on woodworking forums or at clubs and guilds. You'll soon surprise yourself with how much you can do.

CONCLUSION

There are many, many places that you can find patterns for your own woodworking projects. We found plenty of places online. Don't forget your local library as well as home improvement stores like Lowe's and Home Depot. These places carry an extensive line of home woodworking plans for you to complete and wow your family and friends.

Remember the safety procedures we outlined in this book. You cannot be too careful when it comes to keeping yourself safe in your work room. When you work with power tools and even hand tools, accidents can happen that can affect you in horrible ways.

We assume no responsibility in keeping you safe in your work shop. We've given you guidelines and suggestions; the rest is up to you!

The satisfaction you can find when you take up woodworking as a hobby can be amazing. You won't believe the pride you feel as you point out to visitors to your home that you made a piece of furniture yourself.

Just remember to take your time, be safe, and take pride in your work! After all, it was made by you with the two hands you were given. What could be more satisfying than that?

Happy woodworking!

Printed by Libri Plureos GmbH in Hamburg, Germany